Beautiful
Oregon Coast®

"Learn about America in a beautiful way."

Beautiful America Publishing Company

The nation's foremost publisher of quality color photography

Current Books

Alaska
Arizona
Boston
British Columbia
California
California Vol. II
California Coast
California Desert
California Missions
California Mountains
Chicago
Colorado
Dallas
Delaware
Denver
Florida
Georgia
Hawaii
Idaho
Illinois
Indiana
Kentucky
Las Vegas
Los Angeles, 200 Years

Maryland
Massachusetts
Michigan
Michigan Vol. II
Minnesota
Missouri
Montana
Montana Vol. II
Monterey Peninsula
Mt. Hood (Oregon)
Nevada
New Jersey
New York
New York City
New Mexico
Northern California
Northern California Vol. II
North Carolina
North Idaho
Ohio
Oklahoma
Orange County
Oergon
Oregon Vol. II

Oregon Coast
Oregon Country
Pacific Coast
Pennsylvania
Pittsburgh
San Diego
San Francisco
San Juan Islands
Seattle
Tennessee
Texas
Utah
Utah Country
Vancouver U.S.A.
Vermont
Virginia
Volcano, Mt. St. Helens
Washington
Washington Vol. II
Washington, D.C.
Wisconsin
Wyoming
Yosemite National Park

Forthcoming Books

Alabama
Arkansas
Baltimore
Connecticut
Detroit
The Great Lakes
Houston
Kansas

Kauai
Maine
Maui
Mississippi
New England
New Hampshire
North Dakota

Oahu
Phoenix
Rhode Island
Rocky Mountains
South Carolina
South Dakota
West Virginia

Large Format, Hardbound Books

Beautiful America
Beauty of California
Beauty of Oregon

Beauty of Washington
Glory of Nature's Form

Lewis & Clark Country
Western Impressions

Beautiful
Oregon Coast®

Text by Paul M. Lewis

Third Printing, 1980

Published by Beautiful America Publishing Company
P.O. Box 608, Beaverton, Oregon 97075
Robert D. Shangle, Publisher

ISBN 0-915796-20-1 (paperback)
ISBN 0-915796-21-X (hardbound)

PHOTO CREDITS

CONTENTS

Enlarged Prints

Most of the photography in this book is available as photographic enlargements. Send self-addressed, stamped envelope for information. For a complete product catalog, send $1.00.
Beautiful America Publishing Company
P.O. Box 608
Beaverton, Oregon 97075

INTRODUCTION

The trouble with trying to represent, in words, something so rich and varied as the Oregon coastline, is that the attempt must inevitably fail. Any one person's impressions, even those of a long-time coastal resident or an inveterate and tireless beachcomber, are bound to be (1) partial and (2) colored by one's pesonal view of his place in the world. By way of getting himself off the hook, this writer pleads guilty to both (1) and (2). Although I have been an Oregonian for 25 years and have, at one time or another, seen, touched, or trod upon just about every mile of Oregon's glamorous shoreline, I have not unraveled all of its mysteries or discovered all of its charms. And I do indeed look upon this coast's savage beauty as something to be preserved from the incursions of commerce and other inappropriate human activities. Fortunately for me and the world, this matter was taken care of a while back when Oregon reserved nearly the whole 400-mile-plus shore for public use and enjoyment.

Fortunately, too, for me, this commentary is but an accompaniment to the spectacular color photography spread out on the following pages in lavish profusion. The pictures in this book really tell the story very well. The prose just adds an extra dimension to the presentation.

Some of the more esoteric volumes on nature and the wilderness emphasize the need for man to stay away from wild places so that these areas will not be injured by over-use. This point of view certainly has some justification in the case of a fragile system where continual intrusion would mean eventual destruction. But such fears do not apply to the Oregon coast, at least not yet. This is a wilderness that accommodates the proximity of man and his machines, without itself being much affected by that close relationship. The coast highway puts the auto tourist within reach of all the coastal wonders without doing harm to the primitive beauty to be found there.

It's the best of all possible worlds, the philosopher Liebnitz is supposed to have said. Possibly an oversimplification, but it may have some application to Oregon coastal touring. All ranges of explorers have a place there, from the riders of luxurious, temperature-controlled, 12-cylinder gas guzzlers who never leave the security of the highway and the comfort of their car, to the barefoot, backpacking beachcomber who wouldn't be seen in either place. Most of us are somewhere in the middle. We'll rely on motorized transportation when it suits us and trust to feet and legs when we are so minded. Feet and legs are still the best (and sometimes only) way to explore the wilder, remoter headlands, capes, beaches, coves, and bays. That's as it should be, because ease of access would soon cancel out the wild and remote quality of these places. There is, I suppose, a danger that the accessibility provided by the coast highway and other roads will eventually do that anyway. But if the record so far of the people of Oregon and their governments is a good indication, this won't happen. Oregon has shown a level of stewardship that is as magnificent as its magnificent coast. That kind of concern should last for as long as there are Oregonians.

— Paul M. Lewis

ASTORIA —
THE STARTING POINT

San Francisco calls itself the City by the Bay. Astoria might with similar assurance claim to be the Gateway to the Coast. From its corner in northwest Oregon by the mouth of the Columbia, Astoria is the northern starting point for the glamorous coast highway that slithers along the extravagantly spectacular Oregon shore for 375 miles from border to border. But Astoria is also its own point of departure. It has a unique role in the history of the Pacific Coast as the place where American influence first made itself felt. The Spanish, Russians, and British had been busily exploring the seaboard to the south and north when Astoria became an American outpost. The town still preserves evidence of its colorful and sometimes violent past. It's a seafaring place and looks like one, its homes rising in tiers on the hills that climb steeply from a waterfront crowded with fishing and pleasure boats. History is all around you in Astoria. The Astor Column, on a clear day, provides a panoramic view of the river, bay and ocean; it also provides a history lesson in 525 feet of frieze that spirals around the 125-foot-high tower. Museums like the Maritime Museum and the Clatsop County Historical Society Museum display artifacts of the area's past. And in a way the giant new bridge that stretches four miles across the Columbia into Washington is a bridge into the past.

It leads to Fort Columbia, another long-time former coastal sentinel now a Washington state park, just about a half mile away toward Long Beach. In another sense the bridge has at least one foot in the past. It reminds travelers of what it replaced — those marvelous ferries that gave you a choice of crossing that wide river mouth with or without an automobile. Anybody who just wanted to float over the river and back left his car behind, of course, and made the trip for a lot less than it costs to ride that fancy bridge. The bridge is beautiful, a sensible and graceful structure that fits into its magnificent river setting as if it had always been there. But in one or two rivers in Oregon ferries are still getting people and cars from one bank to the other. I hope they keep on doing that for a long time to come. Sometimes the leisurely and inefficient mode of travel is the only way to go.

The Astoria region of the coast is more than minimally furnished with segments that have a connection with history. There's Fort Clatsop, reconstructed from the time when Lewis and Clark officially opened the Oregon tourist era by spending a winter in the neighborhood. It's on the Lewis and Clark River about eight miles south and west of Astoria. The actual fortifications, furniture, and tools — including canoes — of the original encampment have been recreated and designated a national memorial. There is even a museum where Lewis and Clark's westward odyssey is described in detail.

Nearby, and easy to miss like Fort Clatsop, is Fort Stevens. It's approached through the towns of Warrenton and Hammond (unless you're coming in by outrigger canoe). The signs directing drivers to the fort are rather retiring and in at least one case misleading enough to throw you off course. The sign indicates "Fort Stevens" plainly enough but points vaguely at the sky from the juncture of two streets in Warrenton that come together at acute angles. At least one latter-day tourist I know, with a very low psychic quotient, recently had to find Fort Stevens by a process of elimination. But the Warrenton folks are helpful. A store clerk who was approached for help on this occasion sympathized with the befuddled explorer and allowed as how the sign should be more explicit. But I, personally, wouldn't change these little directional eccentricities. They add to the thrill of the unknown that is one of the qualities of this marvelous and still mysterious coastline.

Fort Stevens State Park, when you do reach it, is well worth the struggle. It's on a point of land at the mouth of the Columbia, with miles of broad beaches and sandy flats backed by thick, lush forests, all within the area designated as state park land. It's a big place, and very popular as a north coast beach spot. Fort Stevens is an attraction by itself. There's a spooky fascination in clambering over old gun emplacements and peering into now-retired quarters for military personnel. Battery Russell, I expect, is the main point of interest, because of having been fired upon in World War II by a Japanese submarine whose shells disrupted the contours of several sand dunes. Looking to sea from the parapet of the still-solid and imposing emplacement, one might wonder about the useless daring of the submarine commander and crew.

Another bit of history still survives on the beach. The *Peter Iredale*, a rusty hulk that can be approached at low tide, was once a British vessel that lost, in 1906, an attempt at overland transportation. It beached itself on the Oregon coast, but having no wheels or wings, never got any farther. Although not much of the vessel remains, its longevity as a coastal hulk has been something of a surprise.

The north coast is full of pleasant little towns, some of which may have begun as fishing villages, but which now have turned their primary attention to attracting the tourist. The possibilities of vacations on the Oregon coast have only really begun to be promoted on a large scale in the past few decades, and the north coast settlements of Gearhart and Seaside are cashing in on this relatively new awareness of the infinite variety of the state's shoreline. Gearhart has lately metamorphosed into the golf and convention spot on the coast, with plush facilities that draw the spenders from Portland and other inland towns of the north. Gearhart and nearby Seaside together pull

(Previous Page:) the powerful beacon of Heceta Head lighthouse pierces the late afternoon haze from its eminence on one of Oregon's most-photographed headlands.

(Left:) Freighters lie at anchor in the harbor at Astoria, whose port is one of the busiest on the Pacific Coast.

(Below:) A rocky promontory seen from Arch viewpoint at Boardman State Park bends around to create a sheltered beach.

(Opposite, Above:) Lowering clouds set the stage for one of those patented coastal sunsets as a solitary freighter sails over a hazy sea that reflects the orange-red glow of late afternoon. This scene was photographed from Cape Perpetua.

(Opposite, Below:) Big, wild Cape Lookout, on Oregon's north coast, includes among its several environments a rain forest whose lush growth is typified by this scene.

(Left:) Evening on the beach at Neskowin paints the cliffs with a soft radiance and helps to create a mood of tranquility.

(Below:) Dawn bathes Cannon Beach's Haystack Rock in a soft, golden light.

(Opposite Page:) This piece of driftwood with its antler-like roots seems to personify a beachcombing animal resting on the sun-drenched beach at Cape Meares, in the Three Capes area, north coast.

(Opposite Page:) Evening moonlight bestows a glamorous carpet of silver on the waters of crescent-shaped Short Sands Beach, at Oswald West State Park on the north coast. The small boats ride safely on the sheltered waters of the cove.

(Right.) These weathered pilings on the tidal flats of Astoria's South Jetty area add a lonely, poetic touch to the terrain around them.

(Below:) Cape Blanco Lighthouse stands on a bluff that pushes out into the Pacific farther west than any other Oregon point. The dramatic setting is part of an 1,880-acre park nine miles north of Port Orford.

(Following Two Pages:) The setting sun furnishes the backlighting for a dramatic finale to the day, with Cannon Beach's Needles standing out big, bold and black.

(Left:) The restless sea batters the rocky shore-line at Cape Arago, near Coos Bay.

(Below:) Battle Rock stands a bit out to sea in the right background of this photo taken at high tide from Battle Rock Wayside on the southern coast just south of Port Orford.

(Opposite Page, Above:) Cape Perpetua, on the central coast, takes on a somber aspect under the pale light of a sunset sky.

(Opposite Page, Below:) A sandstone cliff at Otter Crest looks like a medieval battlement as it absorbs the pounding of the surf.

(Following Two Pages:) The offshore rocks and seastacks at Cannon Beach are not only a dramatic part of thee seascape there. They also serve as launching pads for gulls and other seabirds.

(Opposite Page, Above:) A bridge girder carrying the coast highway frames part of this view of the beach at Devil's Elbow State Park. Heceta Head and its lighthouse are in the background.

(Opposite Page, Below:) Boiler Bay, south of Gleneden Beach, looks calm here, but the breakers get pretty wild when the sea is up. The bay was named for a ship's boiler that was washed ashore.

(Right:) A golden sunset at Harris Beach State Park in southern Oregon highlights the sea stacks that dominate the seascape here.

(Below:) Big and little fishing boats and pleasure craft find berths in Newport's spacious harbor.

(Following Page:) A sparkling little waterfall on a coastal stream provides a rain-forest environment for the ferns and mosses that thrive in such a setting.

a lot of visitors to the seashore. Seaside has the best beach on the whole coastline from one point of view. It's a broad, level, and long stretch of sand protected by headlands from the roughest ocean tides. Whenever I walk along the beach here I am reminded of the south Jersey littoral at the edge of another ocean. Seaside has other similarities to some East Coast resorts, with its superabundance of tourist facilities, beach promenade, and carnival atmosphere.

A little back from the coast east of Seaside is Saddle Mountain, a giant coast range mountain exceeded in height only by Mary's Peak. It has some unique aspects that make its inclusion in a north coast itinerary a good idea. It is also a state park, one of those marvelous wildernesses that Oregon has been able to set aside through good fortune and good sense. What makes Saddle Mountain so special? Its incredible profusion of wild flowers in the springtime. There are at least 2,000 species, some so rare they are found only on this mountain, which for some reason — supposedly related to the last Ice Age — has become a sanctuary for species that were isolated on the peak at that time. There are plenty of animals in this mountain park, too; it and the surrounding area are a game reserve that includes deer, black bear, and even elk. A three-mile trail leads from the base to the top of the mountain, and takes about two or three hours to hike. The view from the top — 3,287 feet up — is a visual feast: the Pacific Ocean on the west; the Columbia River mouth, and Astoria, to the north; and all around, snow-capped peaks, like Rainier, Adams, St. Helens, Hood, and Jefferson. Any time of the year Saddle Mountain is a rare treat, an almost mystical piece of volcanic real estate that's very old and very new, like something out of time.

One of the numerous state parks — and one of the biggest — that protect and preserve the coastal wildlands is situated directly south of Seaside. Ecola State Park has some seven miles of ocean frontage that begins at Seaside and reaches to Cannon Beach. The park includes gigantic Tillamook Head from whose high reaches can be seen a long, long stretch of spectacular coastline. One of the park's most charming attractions is Indian Beach, a small, sheltered crescent that is greatly prized by surfers and skin divers. The beach is accessible by a park road, or by trail from The Cove on the north side of the headland at Seaside. The trail is a five-mile switchback up and over Tillamook Head. It's a hefty hike, but worth it. Indian beach and Crescent Beach, another hard sand beach within the park boundaries, are delightful little sheltered places that are prodigal with esthetic delights, for those whose happiness depends on these qualities, and with razor clams, for those who require more substantial satisfaction of their needs.

From Ecola Park's high southern wall another remarkable stretch of shoreline spreads south for several miles. This is Cannon Beach. Though much visited in all

(Following Pages, Left:) A misty dawn makes ghostly shapes out of the boats and dock structures in Charleston's boat basin.
(Following Pages, Above, Right:) Yaquina Head Lighthouse is one of the coast's best-known landmarks.
(Following Pages, Below, Right:) Wild huckleberry thrives in the benign atmosphere of Cape Lookout State Park.

seasons, it is spacious enough to absorb crowds without becoming crowded. Its broad, hard sands encourage a multitude of activities, from horseback and bike riding to car touring (when permitted). But what really makes a place in the world for Cannon Beach is Haystack Rock, by far the mightiest and most awesome of a number of monoliths that stand out to sea just off the beach. At low tide, Haystack has been climbed by adventurous types, some of whom were unable to make the return trip without an assist by Coast Guard helicopter. The usual inhabitants of the big pinnacle are gulls and other seabirds in their thousands.

Cannon Beach ends at Arch Cape, where the character of the coastline begins to change. The broad sweeps of sand are more frequently broken up by great headlands and capes on whose sheer sides the coast highway soars like a magic carpet. The next course on the scenic menu (just south of the Arch Cape tunnel on the coast highway) is beautiful and exotic Oswald West State Park and *its* mountain, Neahkahnie, a big, bold headland with one foot in the sea. On its colossal seaward shoulder the coast highway zooms 530 feet up over the ocean. From viewpoints at the zenith of the climb the traveler can get one of those long views of the coastal breakers so celebrated along the Oregon shore. He can also get a spine-tingling thrill by looking straight down Neahkahnie's perpendicular face to the crashing sea. The 1,700-foot mountain is at the southern edge of Os West Park, and its heavily wooded, rolling hills cloak a myriad of buried-treasure stories and legends of encounters between Indians and pirate crews. Some mysterious markings on rocks near the mountain help keep interest in the treasure stories alive. For those with the time and the energy, a hike up the Neahkahnie Mountain trail to the summit adds a fillip to the enjoyment of the mountain. The walk through Neahkahnie's sumptuous greenery and the view after arriving at the top are more-than-generous reward for the moderate amount of muscle and sweat involved in the effort.

Speaking of sumptuous greenery, some backtracking is in order at this point. Oswald West State Park, which stretches south to Neahkahnie, has been called one of the most beautiful wilderness parks on the coast. Its beauty is exciting and restful (if you will allow that those two qualities can co-exist). The park and its beaches are kept in an entirely natural state, except for an unobtrusive picnic area and camping sites. Its huge spruces and many forms of exotic greenery make it a nature-lover's paradise. The park was designed without roads through its 2,500-plus acres. A piece of wise foresight. Motorized vehicles would be a monstrous intrusion into such an idyllic haven. Cars are parked in areas along the highway, and visitors walk into the park on any of a number of trails. Wheelbarrows are available for campers with gear to transport.

The park's picnic area looks out over a little jewel of a sheltered beach (Short Sands) that stretches in a crescent to a headland. A marine garden along the northern arm of the cove provides opportunity for observance of tidal sea life. And from a trail over the ridge there is a view of offshore sea stacks that are sanctuaries for birds and seals. The truly amazing floral variety of the area is nurtured by the frequent rains that come sweeping in off the ocean, and by the mists that so regularly bathe coastal vegetation in moisture.

BAYS AND BYWAYS

For southbound coastal explorers things take a dramatic turn after Neahkahnie Mountain. Just below the little village of Manzanita the road sweeps sharply east and proceeds to circle peaceful and lovely little Nehalem Bay, running with Chinook and silver salmon in the summer and fall. Coming around to the ocean again it goes through resort towns — bright, friendly communities — before reaching the north shore of Tillamook Bay at Barview. Tillamook Bay is where the action is. A big, deepwater harbor, it does a heavy business in charter fishing. There's a charter pilot in Garibaldi who insists that the bottom fishing here is the best on the Pacific Coast. Maybe. Both sport and commercial fishing yield big harvests of bottom fish and salmon. The big north jetty at Barview is a popular spot for jetty fishing.

Tillamook County, which advertises itself as the "land of trees, cheese, and ocean breeze", has more than 70 miles of stunning coastline from Cape Falcon on the north to Cascade Head on the south to back up the third part of that triad. The coast road, heading inland after skirting the big bay's eastern shore, goes through the "cheesiest" town in Oregon — Tillamook. Tillamook has other reasons for prominence besides its great cheese factory (which is right on the highway). It has a long history in which the early Northwest settlers and the Indians played a part, and it displays artifacts of that history in a fine museum.

The coast highway denies its name at this point and steers a straight inland course through the lush rolling hills and forests of western Tillamook County. Tranquil pastoral scenes open out along the road. All around are rich, green meadows where large herds of Holstein cattle attest to the region's main industry. But Tillamook is also a place where the coastal story continues in a particularly delightful aspect. The coast is still out there somewhere even though Highway 101 ignores it for about 25 miles. So the traveler must avail himself of the "byways" or loop roads that strike out for the coast from the main highway. One such side road begins at Tillamook and can be taken in short spurts or all at once. Called the Three Capes Scenic route, it provides access to three of the coastline's most dramatic and spectacular headlands.

The three capes are, north to south, Meares, Lookout, and Kiwanda. The coastal segment of which they form a part is wild and lonely. The tiny hamlets of Oceanside and Netarts on the Cape Meares road seem to belong to the seacoast as much as the sand and the ocean do. From Tillamook the road edges along the south shore of Tillamook Bay, passing Bayocean Peninsula before turning south to Cape Meares and its state park.

Cape Meares is widely known in the state as the site of the misplaced lighthouse. Late in the last century the federal government selected Cape Lookout for a lighthouse, to help protect coastal shipping. The lighthouse builders, having to hack their way

(Following Two Pages:) Haystack Rock near Cape Kiwanda rises black and brooding out of a sunset sea. The giant seastack at Pacific City is a national wildlife sanctuary.

through virgin wilderness, had a tough time getting their bearings. They never did get them, really, because they and their ox-drawn equipment arrived at Cape Meares, where the lighthouse was built. Nowadays, it probably would have been moved to conform to the original intent. But in 1890, perhaps, the government was less likely to get upset by these little mistakes. Anyway, it was named the Cape Meares Light. No longer used, it is now an historic site.

Cape Meares is the home of another celebrated resident — its Octopus Tree. The tree is an immense, grotesquely beautiful Sitka spruce whose branches spread out horizontally for 60 feet, like a giant candelabra, before turning to the sky. And just down the coast from the wild cape area is Oceanside, an "old world" village. The town's homes have been weathered by the salt mist and they cling to the oceanside cliffs like the seabirds that cluster on Three Arch Rocks, a wildlife refuge just offshore. The birds and a herd of sea lions have made this big, complicated rock pinnacle their ocean resort home.

Between capes Meares and Lookout is about a 10-mile stretch of broad, lonely white-sand beaches. These long, flat shores help give the Three Capes area a stunning variety of terrain and ocean scenery. Netarts Bay, near Cape Lookout, is a good spot for clamming and crabbing. The sand spit that blocks out the Pacific has more than five miles of those silvery sands that touch Cape Lookout itself.

Cape Lookout is one of the stunners of the Oregon Coast. It pushes two miles into the Pacific and by itself is practically a whole ecological system. A basalt finger one-quarter to one-half mile wide, it challenges the sea with sheer cliffs some 600 feet high. The cape's beauty and variety make it a cherised attraction for artists, photographers, and campers. For the campers, Cape Lookout State Park provides extensive, but un-obtrusive, facilities. For the hiker, a long trail from the cape's summit (800 feet) leads to the point and its marvelous coastal views. Barring mists and fog and rain, there's a possible visual shot at Tillamook Head, 42 miles to the north, and of course Cape Meares and Three Arch Rocks. To the south appears Cape Kiwanda and its Haystack Rock wildlife refuge (8 miles), Cascade Head (20 miles), and Cape Foulweather (39 miles).

The cape's natural phenomena include a rain forest comparable to the well-known forests of the Olympic peninsula; one of the only two bird rookeries on the United States Pacific coast; more than 150 species of birds, some of which nest on the sheer walls of the cape; and several animal species, including deer, black bear, raccoon, mink, weasel, flying squirrel, and possibly even bobcat and mountain lion. Indians probably hunted on the cape; Indian artifacts have been found there. The creeks of the cape provide fresh-water fishing. At its southeast corner is one of the most beautiful marine gardens on the coast. Pockets in the sandstone shelf rock contain a quantity of sea urchins which, although animals, look something like begonias (having tentacles up to four inches long). The "flowers" display an infinity of colors, refreshed and in-tensified by the incoming tide. When the tide retreats, the vivid colors are revealed to the observer.

Cape Kiwanda, the southernmost of the three headlands, erupts suddenly after another nine miles or so of fine, flat beaches, pushing out to sea in the dramatic pose of a *lion couchant* (as seen from the south). It provides calm water for a sheltered beach — and brings tourists to little Pacific City which straggles along the shoreline by the cape. This is one of the very few beaches where small boats are able to put out to sea through the breakers. Even the landlubbers from the inland Willamette Valley go down to the sea here as if they had been doing it every day, catching a great variety and number of fish while thus engaged. Salmon, cod, red snapper, flounder, and other bottom fish — all are yielded up to the eager anglers who flock, in the summer, to the great wide swathe of beach here.

Calm water notwithstanding, the tip of the cape is sometimes another matter. The Pacific can be particularly savage here, and its fury has been the subject of many a dramatic photograph when giant storm-driven waves tear at the cape like terrifying demonic forces. Kiwanda is beautiful — and dangerous. Its sheer cliffs pose a real peril to the adventurous climbers who explore them. Lately the Cape Kiwanda and Ocean-side areas have become the locales for a sport that fits in with the scenery in these parts. The sport is hang gliding, and its practitioners go soaring and swooping among the cliffs, dunes, and sea stacks like some outsize primeval bird life that forgot it was extinct.

After the tour of the capes, the car traveler can return to the main coastal highway just by continuing south. And just a few miles farther along is another huge coastal promontory whose basalt rock has been pretty successful in defying the Pacific's best efforts to tear it apart. Cascade Head has lost a little real estate within recent geologic memory, though. In 1934, it gave up about 20 acres of prime pasture land to the sea, creating a considerably sharper profile at that spot and revealing some of the pattern of its construction.

Cascade Head protrudes three miles into the Pacific. Its summit is well over 1,500 feet. The ocean end tops 500 feet and drops off almost vertically into the water. Looked at from one of the roadside stops on either side, Cascade Head looks impressively wild and formidable. It is more than three miles long and carries on its back a forest of Sitka spruce hundreds of years old, with trees of gargantuan proportions. The trees, unfortunately, are but a part of what was once a much more extensive forest that was logged during the years. In 1974, by act of Congress, Cascade Head was declared the country's first Scenic Research Area, which should preserve its rugged beauty, into the far future, from further despoliation.

(Following Page, Above:) South of Astoria the flatlands by the mouth of the Columbia present a picture of lonely desolation.
(Following Page, Below:) The buttercup-like ranunculus finds a place among the lush growth of Cape Lookout State Park.

THE (SOMETIMES) ROLLER-COASTER COASTLINE

The Oregon coast from Cascade Head to Coos Bay is one thing and then another. If chopped up into jigsaw pieces, the segments could be fitted onto the wildly varied shorelines of 10 different countries. The Lincoln City—Waldport stretch is relatively calm and civilized, either gradually descending to long, level beaches or terminating in cliffs and points of dramatic appearance yet manageable proportions. Soon after Waldport, and most of the way to Florence, the Coast Range moves down to the sea in force and the terrain becomes as rugged as any coastline on earth. Huge basaltic headlands push out against the tide, hiding little coves and beaches between them, yielding to the power of the waves only where fissures have been ground out by the sea. The coast highway bravely follows the contours of this wild and intricate shoreline, sometimes lifting high up over the Pacific on a sheer cliff face, then zooming down and around a little bay almost at eye level. In the tortured dance it must do to get through this obstacle course, it is a wriggling snake, a pirouetting ballerina, an undulating ribbon. At Florence, and all the way to Coos Bay-North Bend the shoreline becomes a desert. For 40 miles, sand dunes roll and undulate along the shore, reaching inland one to three miles to the highway.

Below Cascade Head the beaches are broad, long, and inviting. Such an area is ripe for tourist development, and that has been going on at a rapid pace since World War II. Long known as the "Twenty Miracle Miles" through tourist promotions, it was actually something less than that until in 1964 the five small towns in the area combined into one 5½-mile-long "metropolis" called Lincoln City and in the process cleaned up the visual blight that had been driving away more tourists than otherwise. Lincoln City has its eye on the main chance and goes after the tourist dollar as unre-

(Preceding Page, Above:) A calm sea and congregating seabirds add up to an idyllic scene in this sunset view at Bandon.

(Preceding Page, Below:) Looking south from the summit of Cape Perpetua, the observer can gaze at many miles of magnificent coastline.

servedly as any resort town. But now it's a pleasant center of activity for visitors to the central coast. With all the town's businesslike air and spiffy good looks, the folks there haven't lost their sense of humor. On a recent visit I spotted this sign in front of a main street business: "Bigotry is an Italian Redwood." The charming Siletz River and its bay are features of the Lincoln City area.

A couple of miles farther along is the tiny hamlet of Gleneden Beach, on Siletz Bay. Salishan Lodge, the Oregon coast's most ambitious resort complex, sprawls on the other side of the highway. Salishan is an immense place on a height overlooking the bay. It is completely self-sufficient, and conceived in impeccable taste that respects the scenic integrity of its coastal setting. But the beaches are still the main attraction on this part of the coast. Beachcombing has been raised to a high art here, and rewards are ample for the wily and persistent. The knowledgeable searcher starts early in the day, with the outgoing tide. He may be looking for anything imaginable and that is what he may find. The most popular items are agates and glass floats, but the sea may deposit a variety of treasures on the shore, be they driftwood, man-made articles from boots to boats, or some of the sea's own creations, alive and dead. The prize, whatever it is, acquires great value because it is a gift from the sea.

A sea creature that does not normally get washed onto the shore is the whale. When whales migrate, Oregonians and anyone else interested congregate on the shore to watch them pass on their coastal journey. One of the best places for such opportunities is at Boiler Bay Wayside just south of Gleneden Beach. The writer, whale-watching recently at Boiler Bay, among a multitude of persons similarly occupied, began to have doubts whether he was the watcher or the watchee. The multitude of spouting mammals passing by seemed to be maneuvering for a better look at the strange shore-bound mammals waving and shouting from the rocky prominence. The little cove of Boiler Bay is heavily pummeled when the ocean takes a notion, but that is not how it got its name. As a sign at the wayside informs you, a ship's boiler was washed ashore here and is still partly visible at low tide.

Depoe Bay, just south, is one of the coast's big little towns. It's really quite small physically, but looms large in coastal activity, whether of the landlubber or seafaring kind. It's built on rocky coastal cliffs, and its tiny harbor is entered through a narrow corridor that leads in from the open sea. The harbor is known as "The Hole" by the residents, and a bridge carries the coast highway across its entrance. The size of the

(Following Pages, Above, Left:) The beach cliffs and rock islands at Bandon add to the beauty and interest of this area south of Coos Bay.

(Following Pages, Below, Left:) Geisel Wayside seven miles north of Gold Beach is a fine vantage point for observing and photographing a particularly delightful part of the coastal profile.

(Following Pages, Above, Right:) The view north from Boardman State Park near Brookings offers a sumptuous vista of Oregon's intricate southern coastline.

(Following Pages, Below, Right:) Giant Cape Lookout provides sheltered waters for fishing boats and a long view of the surrounding beaches.

boats that use the bay is somewhat limited by the smallness of the harbor and the 50-foot (mean high water) clearance of the bridge. But an exhuberant and colorful collection of fishing boats and pleasure craft can be seen any day in this snug little haven. Depoe Bay is of course quite tourist-oriented, but with restraint. It is one of the coastal towns where artists gather, and some of their work can be purchased in shops. One of the interesting attractions just north of the bay bridge is the little aquarium where specimens of Pacific coast sea life are displayed. The big laugh-getters are the seals and their frantic antics to get a handout from aquarium visitors. They slap the water, bark, do arabesques, tap the low glass partition, or just rivet a likely prospect with a sad gaze. They're a knowing bunch of comedians who constantly case the entrance (where the seal food is purchased) and know in advance who is worth their attention by the time people arrive at their tank.

A couple of miles south of Depoe Bay, Otter Crest Wayside (on a short loop road) provides one of those patented views of the coastline that stun the senses. The viewpoint is on Cape Foulweather 500 feet above the sea. The view to the south seems to open up endlessly, and as far as the eye can see the rhythmic breakers move up to the shore and out again. The impact of the magnificent ocean panorama changes with the weather and the time of day. On a mildly blustery, mostly clear day such as the one I experienced on a recent spring visit to the cape, the ocean far below and far out to the horizon takes on the look of a great metallic plate. It reminded me that day of a shimmering carpet of chain mail, the surface stippled but not disturbed enough to raise whitecaps. Here and there the cottony little clouds in the afternoon sky threw black shadows down into the water-holes in the ocean that moved quickly over the surface.

The Devil's Punchbowl just south of Cape Foulweather is another of those cave-like creations of the relentless ocean, where the rocky shelf has been undercut to the extent that the roof falls in. The resulting chamber is entered at several points by the sea, which in angry moods turns into roiling foam as it beats against the rock walls, spewing high into the air and drenching unwary onlookers on the viewpoint above.

Agate Beach comes along in a few miles. On the northern outskirts of Newport, it is a mecca for — who else? — agate hunters, the breed of rockhounds who do their beachcombing with head down, gazing with fierce concentration at the wet sands in the sure knowledge that the sea will inevitably yield up to them some of her gemstone treasures. Agate Beach is only one of many Oregon beaches on the middle coast that specialize in the colorful bits of rock that come in an infinite variety of pattern and color. But this beach is also one of the most walkable — long, wide, level, and uncluttered. A beautiful piece of the shoreline in a visually sumptuous setting.

(Opposite Page:) Showy rhododendron blooms brighten a parcel of dense forest on Cape Kiwanda, in the Three Capes area.

(Following Page, Above:) Looking south from below Cannon Beach, this view shows a typically deserted stretch of shoreline where the white sands and the sea meet in lonely embrace.

(Following Page, Below:) Netarts Bay, sheltered from the sea by a long sandspit, is a beautiful little body of water between capes Meares and Lookout.

(Preceding Page:) A lone seagull silhouetted in the gathering dusk has the best possible viewpoint atop a Cannon Beach seastack as the restless Pacific pounds his rocky perch.

(Left:) These stumps near Neskowin are remnants of an ancient forest doomed when the sea invaded its territory.

(Below:) Depoe Bay's snug little harbor has a slit-like entrance that locks out the pounding ocean.

(Opposite Page, Above:) Tillamook Light-house appears all alone in this dark blue scene with clouds obscuring all but a yellow streak from the setting sun.

(Opposite Page, Below:) Lush greenery surrounds a moss-covered rock at Hebo Lake on Hebo Mountain near Pacific City on the north coast.

(Opposite Page:) The Devil's Punch Bowl at Otter Crest is aptly named. The sea enters holes in the rock shelf at several points, and at times its wild churning sends spray high into the air.

(Right:) Humbug Mountain, on the southern coast, rises up from the sea more than 1,700 feet. The mountain and its vicinity have become a popular vacation area.

(Below:) The beach near Cape Sebastian, below Gold Beach, is guarded by a multitude of offshore rocks that add interest to the sandy shoreline.

(Following Two Pages:) The view south from Ecola State Park's Tillamook Head is long and spectacular, including Cannon Beach with its giant offshore rocks, and beyond.

(Left:) A small stream adds a fresh beauty to this forest scene in the Coast Range.

(Below:) Otter Crest is a particularly popular and scenic spot on the Oregon Coast, with a resort that blends well with the surrounding beauty.

(Opposite:) The darkening seascape catches an array of fishing boats standing offshore

(Opposite Page, Above:) Cape Arago Lighthouse at Sunset Bay looks small and lonely as its light works bravely to pierce the thick Pacific fog.

(Opposite Page, Below:) Agate Beach presents a face of calm beauty in the late afternoon, with its cliffside turned golden by the setting sun.

(Right:) Great stacks of driftwood cover many of Oregon's beaches. This cove, with its hoard of sea litter, is near Depoe Bay.

(Below:) Moonlight dusts the breakers with silver in this night scene taken on Neah-kahnie Mountain on the north coast. Nehalem Bay can be seen dimly in the far background.

(Opposite Page:) The graceful highway bridge at Newport is one of many beautiful structures that carry the coast road over bays, rivers, and other natural barriers.

(Right:) Bandon Lighthouse, no longer in use, appears to be waiting for a call back to service.

(Below:) Cape Kiwanda's Haystack Rock lends its impressive bulk to the wild and primitive seascape at the village of Pacific City on the north coast.

(Following Page, Above:) This assortment of seastacks and pinnacles at Bandon Beach seems to have been created solely for the benefit of the seagull lording it over everything from his spiky eminence in the center.

(Following Page, Below:) The green and forested face of Neahkahnie Mountain sets off beautiful Short Sands Beach in Oswald West State Park.

Newport is one of the three big towns on the Oregon coast, the other two being Astoria and Coos Bay. The town is magnificently situated on the north shore of Yaquina Bay, crossed by the coast highway on one of the many graceful spans that carry the road across river mouths and bays. The harbor is one of the busiest in the state, crowded with big and little fishing craft, commercial and private. Newport was long a "society" resort for vacationing Oregonians, but now its modern main street (the coast highway) and ocean-front motels beckon to the tourist and inlanders who want to combine the excitement of the coast with the many "civilized" diversions that this attractive town can offer. Newport's waterfront on the bay is the place where the old town still lives. There are several blocks of docks, fish-processing facilities, restaurants, bars, shops, and battered old buildings that bear witness to a time not so long ago when the Newport waterfront was a shade wilder than it is now. Across the bay is the Marine Science Center of Oregon State University, open to the public during visiting hours.

The profile of the shoreline is generally straight, without the barriers of headlands, all the way to Waldport, about 15 miles. One could hike this stretch with ease, providing he's prepared to do some wading at places where streams of various sizes meander along the sand on their way to mother ocean. Among the features that make this an interesting stretch to explore are the sea stacks and other offshore pinnacles along the way. Seal Rock, one of the better known of these rock structures, offers beach explorers a chance, at low tide, to clamber up the sides, or just to investigate the tide pools around its base.

Waldport is a tiny coastal community whose charming setting on the south shore of Alsea Bay is being discovered by more and more inland valley dwellers. So Waldport and the nearby coastal hills are steadily losing some of their "sleepy hamlet" look. The area has long been a favorite gathering place for those who seek the prizes of the sea. The broad estuarial waters are rich fishing and crabbing grounds. The clam diggers are active here, too.

Some eight more miles south is Yachats, one of the coast's more delightfully situated little (but growing) communities. Straddling the little Yachats River, it sits amid a magnificent setting embracing the river, the ocean, the great wall of Cape Perpetua on the south, and an enormous coastal forest — the Siuslaw National Forest — that covers most of the coast south beyond Reedsport. Yachats is a splendid place to watch the ocean raise hell. A great shelf of volcanic rock on the north shore pushes into the tireless surf. By standing out on this rock one can with safety achieve an intimate experience of the thud of the waves as they batter and tear at the land. An angry sea will

(Following Pages, Left:) A coastal mountain stream does its beautiful best in the cool recesses of a rain forest.

(Following Pages, Upper Right:) Yaquina Head and its lighthouse are bathed in the late afternoon glow, in this view from Agate Beach.

(Following Pages, Lower Right:) The stark sandstone cliffs of Cape Kiwanda are constantly battered by the crashing waves of the Pacific.

also put on a rousing show in the little river bay, tearing away at the rocky, sandy banks. On the south side the beach is broad and sandy, one of the good agate hunting beaches.

At the southern edge of Yachats the coast and the road that follows it became a crazy jumble of swoops and swerves, hairpin turns, deep dives, and sudden climbs — a breathtaking career that lasts to within a few miles of Florence, 26 miles south. A big reason for this state of affairs is Cape Perpetua, a giant headland from whose 800-foot summit the prospect is dazzling. The shoreline seems to extend into infinity to the north and south, broken by headlands and ornamented by giant offshore rocks. A two-mile road from the base of the cape reaches this lofty viewpoint, making it easily attainable by the auto tourist.

The United States Forest Service maintains an information center at Cape Perpetua, offering films and other materials detailing the coastal flora and fauna of the cape area. The center, set back and up from the highway, is open to the public every day during the season, with rangers on duty. Trails wander out to various points of interest in Neptune State Park, through thick rain forest with lush shrubbery like salal, cow parsnip, wild lily-of-the-valley, huckleberry, and rhododendron. The shoreline here is one of the most forbidding on the coast — great, basaltic fingers chewed at by the sea and pocked with tide pools swarming with minute sea life. One of the trails leads down the steep side of a rock cliff to the Devil's Churn, a fascinating and terrifying cleft gouged into the bowels of the cape over incalculable time. The fascinating and terrifying part comes when you sit on the edge of this awesome fissure, especially when the sea is riled up. You can look down and watch the mad waves come pounding in, compressed into writhing foam in the narrow space. You can feel the power in those tons and tons of water when they hit with a thud. The withdrawing tide is just as impressive. As it rushes back out of the long slot there is a screech like that of an elevated train struggling around a curve in the track. Other trails lead to overlooks with views of spouting horns and tide pools, through thick spruce forests and out along the cliff rim set with picnic areas and benches for ocean-gazing. One could spend many weeks in this wonderland without exhausting its fascination.

A few more miles farther along, Heceta Head is another impressive coastal barrier. The head and its lighthouse are extremely popular with vacationers and photographers. From nearby Sea Lion Point, just south, Heceta Head has been photographed endlessly. The head guards a snug little cove and sandy beach in Devil's Elbow State Park; giant sea stacks stand close to the beach — one near enough to be climbed by the nerveless and brainless (sea birds do their own brand of acrobatics on the ones out of reach of wingless creatures); a campground and beach adjoins on the north (Washburne State Park). So Heceta Head is a complete little vacationland, with a protected beach for swimming, surfing, fishing, and agate hunting, caves and offshore rocks to excite the imagination, a forest, and a working lighthouse to admire close up via a short trail. The level area of the lighthouse grounds offers a superb panorama of the whole beach area.

DUNES, DUNES, BEAUTIFUL DUNES

Between Florence and Coos Bay is a part of the shoreline that is unique in a different way from most of the Oregon coast. A long strip — for more than 40 miles — of gigantic dunes undulates from the ocean inland up to three miles. In 1972 the area was designated the Oregon Dunes National Recreation Area, giving it a protected status. The dunes are, to say the least, startling when first seen. Some of them are several hundred feet high and are ideal for riding in dune buggies, contraptions with outsize tires that zip up and down and around the mountains of sand to provide paying passengers with a thrilling, but safe, diversion. But the best way to appreciate and enjoy the dunes, for my money, is to get out and walk. What seems, at a brief glance, to be nothing but sand, turns out to have a surprising variety of features.

One of the places to get acquainted with some of this terrain is at Honeyman State Park, a few miles south of Florence. Honeyman has some big freshwater lakes like Cleawox and Woahink, forests that can be explored by trail, and many kinds of wildlife, including deer. Nearby are the big fishing lakes of Siltcoos and Tahkenitch. The smaller pockets of fresh water that gather in the valleys of some dune areas are interesting, too, for the very fact that they are there. The water in these "oases" is much warmer than the ocean water, and the hollows where it gathers are protected from the wind by the sandy hills — so the bigger ones are great places for swimming, or even surfing.

But there is a Pacific Ocean here, too, even if the dunes seem to have stolen some of its thunder. The combination of sand dunes edged with little forests of wind-blown trees and dotted with little lakes here and there, and the lonely, isolated beaches make this terrain a very special and idyllic part of the world. The hum of fast traffic is nearby (the coast highway is right over the next sand dune) yet this little Sahara is galaxies removed from it in aspect and mood. There are lots of "secret" places where there's nobody but you, where you can be the emperor of the universe without undue harassment from your subjects, be they sand fleas or seagulls. One of my favorite Shangri-las is Carter Lake, just south of Siltcoos. The U.S. Forest Service has a little campground there, back in a lovely little fringe of forest between the lake and the dunes. The lake itself begins as a narrow finger near the highway, then broadens into a sparkling, forest-bordered swimming and fishing hole, with a little beach in a clearing near the camp ground. A trail leads up and out of the campground through the forest to the edge of the dunes. From there it's less than a mile to the beach, over and around the mountains of sand, through clumps of sedge grass and salal, wading (if you wish) in glittery little

(Following Two Pages:) The tortured shapes of driftwood scattered along the beaches near Cape Sebastian rival the intricate sculpturing of the offshore rock structures.

lakes that bar your way, sitting or lying on the lee side of a hillock of sand and in the calm of this delicious little hollow letting the sun toast you as you shuck most of your clothing. The ocean shore, when you do reach it, is almost as lonely. You may see one or two other beach wanderers poking among the driftwood, but that's just enough to put your mind at ease in case you had started to think you were the last person left on earth.

Winchester Bay, about halfway along the dunes country at Reedsport, is known as one of the finest of the countless fine fishing waters along the Oregon coast. The marina at Salmon Harbor is a magnet for sport fishermen in the summer, especially when the salmon gather for their swim up the Umpqua River. One of the largest and most interesting of the coastal state parks touches the bay's south shore and spreads south, with four miles of ocean frontage. Umpqua Lighthouse State Park has a marvelous variety of environments within or bordering its 2,700-plus acres. The bay, the river, the ocean, and two beautiful lakes, accompanied by forests and dunes, make this park a recreational paradise. And, yes, there's the Umpqua Lighthouse, too. One of the six working lighthouses of the Oregon coast, it is also one of the most picturesque.

The north shore of Coos Bay is about 16 miles distant. This lonely terrain is marvelous hiking and backpacking country, whether on the beach itself, in the Umpqua River area around Reedsport, and in the Umpqua Dunes Scenic Area near the Ten Mile Lakes. Abundant wildlife is typical of the whole dunes strip. Early-morning explorers may discover animal tracks, especially in and around wooded areas. Some of the lakes are home for beaver and migratory waterfowl. Deer and raccoon are common. And the ubiquitous seagulls and other shore birds hold their conventions here in their usual large numbers.

The domain of the dunes comes to an end at Coos Bay. Although the southern coast has its dunes, it is generally a different kind of shore, and just as fascinating. But after one spends some time in the dunes country and has recovered from the very wonder of this strange terrain, he may make a resolution to come back to it again soon. Such is the strong attraction of the Oregon Dunes.

THE LONELY AND LOVELY SOUTH COAST

It used to be that the only way to get to and from Oregon's southern shores was by boat. But that was a while back. Now there are some roads to supplement the ocean and the rivers. But things are still pretty wild. The coast highway runs along the shoreline, but after Bandon, roads into the hinterland are nonexistent. The thick forests of the Siskiyou Mountains effectively discourage vehicular travel. So human habitation of this coast is still rather light, although the population is increasing as more and more visitors, especially Californians, discover this unique seascape.

It might seem anomalous, in depicting a lonely coastline, to start with Oregon's most populous coastal town. But Coos Bay is a kind of anchor point for the little south coast communities, and an important part of the scene. The big, beautiful, deep-water bay is about 15 miles in area, negotiated by big lumber freighters. Coos Bay claims that it is the world's largest lumber shipping port. If it isn't, it ought to be. Coos Bay's history is a history of coastal logging that began in earnest in the last century to fill the needs of California's cities and towns.

The bay is crossed by the mile-long McCullough Bridge, another one of those graceful coastal spans that seem to be almost a natural part of the setting. North Bend, contiguous with Coos Bay, is a lumber town like its sister city, but that's as far as the identity business goes. North Bend remains very much itself and prefers it that way, even though there's no geographical separation. A road that follows the south shore of the bay leads to Charleston, where the bay meets the sea. Charleston has its own snug little harbor, and because it's across a bridge from Coos Bay seems to be in another world entirely. It's a very active fishing community, and charter fishing is a big business. It has lots of marina facilities for pleasure fishing. These waters produce abundant tuna, striped bass, shad, and salmon, and the bay itself is good hunting ground for shellfish.

Charleston is also a good takeoff point for shorewatchers. Close by are three of Oregon's state parks that qualify as scenic spectaculars. They are within a mile or so of each other but each has a distinctive character. On the north is Sunset Bay State Park, just past the Cape Arago Lighthouse. Here a beautiful little natural bay is enclosed by steep sandstone bluffs.

Shore Acres State Park, next down the line, contains more than 680 acres, including some bizarre and beautiful shoreline. Its seaward-tilted sandstone wall, undercut by the waves, is often the setting for a magnificent show of the kind not seen anywhere else. When the sea is showing its muscle, the waves spray fifty feet into the air as they fling themselves against the tilted slabs.

(Following Page, Above:) A coastal explorer standing atop Cape Meares on the north coast is treated to a long and glamorous view looking south to Cape Lookout.
(Following Page, Below:) A calm sea, a fishing boat, and brilliant moonlight create a dreamy mood in this scene off Cape Blanco on the south coast.

The southernmost of the three parks is Cape Arago, which projects into the ocean in such a way as to form a north and south bay. Since the south bay is protected from the prevailing north winds of summer, it is ideal as a bathing beach. A seaward arm of the cape forms a mighty barrier to the ocean and makes it possible for small boats to use the south bay as a starting point for ocean fishing. An observation shelter on the bluff affords a view of this extremely rugged and beautiful coastline and sometimes a look at boats standing out to sea or in the cove, awaiting the best tide for making the run into the safety of the Coos Bay harbors.

The county road that leads to these three magnificent parks scuttles along a remote and isolated shoreline known as the Seven Devils Coast. For about 16 miles it follows a wandering course through this wild country until connecting with the main highway eight miles above Bandon. Outlet roads lead to the battered coastal cliffs and rocky beaches. It's a rich area for rockhounds or just plain scavenger types. Whether you're looking for bright-colored rocks, agates, petrified wood, or nothing at all, the Seven Devils beaches give you something extra: a sense of being a part of nature that is wild and free, where man is just another creature in a world of equals.

Bandon-by-the-Sea is also by the mouth of the Coquille River, so has a role in two watery worlds. Just north of town, for example, Bullards Beach State Park has both ocean beach and frontage on the Coquille estuary. Bandon itself has some attractive beach terrain with the added interest of offshore rock pinnacles. A loop road that curves through town and out along the bluffs to the south provides a vantage point for appreciation of the charm and variety of the Bandon seascape.

Bandon to Cape Blanco junction is about 22 miles on the coast highway, but since the road takes an inland course through this lush, rolling terrain, there's not much ocean scenery to be admired. Cape Blanco is where the coastal story resumes. The cape and its lighthouse are reached by a six-mile side road through a particularly wild, lonely, and windy part of the earth. The lighthouse was built in 1870 and still lights the night to warn ship captains of coastal hazards. Cape Blanco sticks out farther west than any other point along the coast, so it would seem a good spot to operate a warning beacon.

Coos Bay-North Bend and Coquille have their myrtlewood groves, and a thriving industry turns out hand-tooled articles from this rare, beautifully grained wood; Bandon is celebrated as a cranberry center, with its bright red cranberry bogs surrounding the town. Port Orford, six miles below Cape Blanco, is the hub of Port Orford cedar country. This aromatic cedar, like the myrtlewood farther north, grows only on the

(Preceding Page, Above:) Saddle Mountain, east of Seaside in the north Coast Range, is a botanist's paradise. Its incredible profusion of wild flowers in the springtime make it a unique area.

(Preceding Page, Below:) The wreck of the Peter Iredale *is a popular attraction on the beach at Fort Stevens State Park south of Astoria.*

Oregon coast and inland for about 30 miles. The wood is durable as well as sweet-smelling, and has many uses as a component of a variety of products, from sailing ships to high-quality furniture. The town of Port Orford itself became a shipping port for the cedar in the early days of the coastal lumber trade, but in 1851 a ruckus occurred on the beach that gave Port Orford a more definitive place in Oregon history. Battle Rock, south of town, was the scene of a siege of nine gold prospectors by Coquille Indians. The natives were driven off, and all the prospectors escaped up the coast, but Battle Rock, the remains of a coastal headland, has become more than just an interesting place to climb and take in the view. The view is, by all odds, worth getting besieged by Indians; from the crest of the rock a seascape of extraordinary beauty spreads out before the observer.

Port Orford achieved another slice of notoriety on account of the famous and mysterious "Port Orford Meteorite," a colossal rock mass supposed to have fallen 40 miles east of the town in the early 1860s. A government geologist claimed to have discovered it and estimated its weight at 22,000 tons. But in a century of searching since then it has never been located. The "lost meteorite" is not too surprising, considering the wild and rugged terrain of the Siskiyou Mountains in this part of Oregon.

Battle Rock is big, but another "rock" six miles south is bigger, and is the center-piece of a state park which bears its name. Humbug Mountain rises like a giant projectile 1,750 feet out of the sea. The mountain and its park comprise more than 1,800 acres of virgin forest, stretches of sandy beach, shaded camping area, and hiking trails. One trail winds up to the top of Humbug Mountain itself.

The mild, rainy climate of the south coast between Port Orford and Gold Beach produces a lush "rain forest" type of growth, similar to the vegetation of the tropics. This is observable in the giant size of long-lived trees, the quantity of moss, and the outsize dimensions of fern and other forest undergrowth. A "prehistoric garden" set up in such a forest eight miles south of Humbug projects a realistic picture of a long-ago era with its life-like dinosaurs and other prehistoric beasts standing around as if ready to roam the area just as they used to do.

Another 20 miles down the coast highway brings the traveler to Gold Beach, whose name would seem to imply the presence of the precious mineral in its beach sand. But Gold Beach does its prospecting these days for tourists, and is admirably equipped for this activity. For one thing, it is at the mouth of one of Oregon's wildest and most beautiful rivers — the Rogue. This circumstance draws many fishermen and un-fishermen who want to fish the Rogue or just take a boat trip on it. The Rogue River mail boat — just about the last of its kind — begins its upriver run from Wedderburn, a point one mile north of downtown Gold Beach. The 32-mile trip to Agness, a village deep in the forest, is accomplished every day during the summer and fall, and

(Following Page, Above:) Oswald West State Park, considered one of the most beautiful in the state, has beaches and forests that remain nearly undisturbed by man.
(Following Page, Below:) Sunset Bay State Park, near Coos Bay, has a charming little natural bay protected from the ocean by sandstone cliffs.

three times a week from November to May. The big, powerful mail boats really do deliver the mail to back country points along the river, but anybody with the price of a ride can go along too. It's a day-long excursion through the extravagantly beautiful canyon country of the lower Rogue, with many glimpses of wild life along the way. A longer, 52-mile ride that penetrates to the "wild river" stretches is also available.

A few miles down the coast from Gold Beach is Cape Sebastian State Park, a typical example of the stunning coastal scenery concentrated between Gold Beach and Brookings. The park area covers more than 1,000 acres combining forest land, and the gorgeous blooms (in season) of rhododendron, blue ceanothus, wild azaleas, and blue iris. The view from the 728-foot-high cape is particularly grand, spiced by the offshore seastacks.

Before the modern coastal highway was built along the south shore, travelers had to brave a bad, old, twisty road that looped up and down and around the bluffs. From Pistol River to Brookings the old road is still available for those who want an extra measure of scenic delights. The regular highway has scenery enough in this 18-mile stretch, including the spectacular, 350-foot-high Thomas Creek Bridge, higher than the Golden Gate Bridge. There are many points of access to the beach, and view points where the coastal drama can provide a visual experience beyond description. One of these is at Cape Ferrelo, just north of Harris Beach State Park. Harris Beach park, the most southerly state campground, has its own scenic vantage point on Harris Butte. On the crest of the Butte one can take in a 24-mile coastal curve from Cape Ferrelo south to California's Point St. George, with its thunderous surf and huge rock islands just offshore.

Harris Beach State Park competes for attention in this coastal corner with Azalea State Park and the town of Brookings, on the mouth of the Chetco River. Azalea park and Brookings combine in May for an azalea festival, the highlight of a practically year-round flowery spectacle made possible by Brookings' mild climate. Besides the flowers, there's fishing for the plentiful salmon and steelhead in the river, and surf and rock fishing on the beaches.

There's an apt French expression that would characterize the scenic riches nature has so prodigally strewn about Oregon's south coast. There's an *embarras de choix* — you don't know where to look next. Not only are there magnificent beaches, but miles of uplifted cliffs fronting the beaches. These rugged terraces with their vertical walls define and integrate the seascape. Offshore, the massive sea stacks and rock islands intrigue the observer; you want somehow to join the swarming colonies of seabirds out there and get a backward look at the ragged, curving shoreline.

It's a feast of the senses that would be considered extraordinary, were not all this just icing on the cake. From Astoria to the California border such treats are legion. If there is anywhere in the world where nature has cooked up a banquet of masterpieces, it is most certainly the unforgettable Oregon coast.

(Preceding Page:) Beach grass, sand, and offshore rocks merge in an interesting blend of textures near Brookings on the south coast.